Who Was Stan Lee?

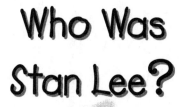

Who Was Stan Lee?

by Geoff Edgers

illustrated by John Hinderliter

Penguin Workshop

To my favorite superhero, Cal. For saving the day—GE

For Tessa, who wants to be an artist—JH

PENGUIN WORKSHOP
An Imprint of Penguin Random House LLC, New York

If you purchased this book without a cover, you should be aware that this book is stolen property. It was reported as "unsold and destroyed" to the publisher, and neither the author nor the publisher has received any payment for this "stripped book."

Visit us online at www.penguinrandomhouse.com.

Library of Congress Control Number: 2014958194

ISBN 9780448482361   20 19

Contents

Who Was
Stan Lee?

Martin Goodman, the publisher of Timely Comics in New York City, didn't know what to do with the teenager. But the boy was his wife's cousin and she had asked Goodman to hire him.

So, just like that, Stanley Martin Lieber was working in the middle of the Golden Age of Comics. As a boy, Stan spent hours curled up with comic books. Now, he was part of that world!

Superheroes were everywhere at Timely. The Human Torch fought bad guys with fire. Namor the Sub-Mariner could fly and breathe underwater, and he was as strong as a thousand men. Captain America began life as a scrawny art student, but turned into a superhero after the US government recruited him for the Super Soldier project.

At first, Stan kept to himself. The artists at Timely were a little scary. They were all older, smoked big cigars, and yelled at each other all day long. What was there for a seventeen-year-old kid from the Bronx to do?

Young Stanley Lieber ran to the deli for sandwiches at lunchtime and made sure the artists' inkwells were full. But he wasn't going to waste a lifetime fetching coffee and answering phones. He had dreams. He was a writer. He wanted to tell stories and maybe someday write the great American novel.

One day, two of Timely Comics' top managers both got angry and quit their jobs. Mr. Goodman needed someone to run the office while he was taking naps or playing golf. He called Stan over and offered him the job.

That's when Stanley Lieber became Stan Lee. In the next half century, he would help create some of America's most famous superheroes, including Spider-Man, Iron Man, Hulk, and the X-Men. He wasn't the only person who made comic books for a living, but Stan Lee was the best.

Chapter 1
Growing Up

Stanley Lieber was born on December 28, 1922, in New York City.

His father, Jack, and mother, Celia, were immigrants from Romania who lived in a tiny apartment. Like millions of people, they had come to the United States with dreams of a better life. They wanted to start a family and buy a house.

Jack got a job cutting fabric at a dress factory. He was paid very little and worked long hours. Celia stayed home and took care of Stan. By the time Stanley was six, the Great Depression had begun. Millions of people lost their jobs, including Stan's father.

Now the family struggled to pay bills. Jack and Celia began to argue. Stan worried whenever his parents argued. He loved his parents and didn't want them to fight.

The Lieber family moved to an even smaller apartment. Jack and Celia had to sleep on a cot in the living room. There was only one tiny window, and it faced a brick wall.

Stan's mother wanted him to finish school quickly so he could go to work to help the family. She pushed Stan to study hard, and he did. He ended up skipping a few grades, which meant that he was always the youngest in his class. He sometimes struggled to make friends.

THE GREAT DEPRESSION

THE GREAT DEPRESSION STARTED ON OCTOBER 29, 1929, WHEN THE STOCK MARKET CRASHED, CAUSING MANY BANKS AND INDUSTRIES TO SHUT DOWN. IT WAS THE WORST ECONOMIC CRISIS OF MODERN TIMES. UNEMPLOYMENT PEAKED IN 1933, WHEN ONE-QUARTER OF ALL AMERICANS WERE OUT OF WORK AND COULD NOT FIND JOBS.

PRESIDENT HERBERT HOOVER'S NAME BECAME LINKED TO THE HARDSHIPS THAT MANY PEOPLE FACED. "HOOVERVILLES"—TOWNS MADE UP OF TENTS AND SHACKS BUILT BY PEOPLE WHO HAD NO OTHER PLACE TO LIVE—POPPED UP EVERYWHERE. SOUP WAS CALLED "HOOVER STEW."

THE GREAT DEPRESSION LASTED NEARLY TEN YEARS. IT AFFECTED NOT ONLY THE UNITED STATES BUT COUNTRIES ALL AROUND THE WORLD.

Stan's favorite teacher was Leon B. Ginsberg, Jr.
Mr. Ginsberg had a great sense of humor and
always told a funny story to make his point. Stan
learned that people remember stories if they are
told with a sense of humor.

As a boy, Stan loved to write. He also loved to read—even if it was just the label of a ketchup bottle on the kitchen table! In fact, Stan always had a book or magazine with him at meals. The Hardy Boys was one of his favorite book series. Two adventurous brothers,

Frank and Joe Hardy, were the heroes of the books. Stan also loved to draw. He wasn't the best artist, but that didn't matter. Drawing helped Stan tell his stories.

During the summers, many New York boys went to camps outside the city. But the Liebers couldn't afford to send Stan away to camp. Instead, Stan stayed home and read. Stan's mother even bought him a stand to keep his books upright on the table while he ate.

Whenever he could afford a ticket, Stan loved to go to the movies. There were five theaters to choose from near his apartment. They showed movies like *Frankenstein*, *Sherlock Holmes*, and *King Kong*. Stan daydreamed of being like Errol Flynn, the handsome actor who starred as Robin Hood.

When Stan was nine, his brother, Larry, was born. As Stan got older, the family really needed him to pitch in and get a job.

YOUNG STAN'S FAVORITE AUTHORS

H. G. WELLS (1866-1946) GREW UP IN ENGLAND AND WAS KNOWN AS "THE FATHER OF SCIENCE FICTION." HIS MOST FAMOUS BOOK, *THE WAR OF THE WORLDS*, WAS ABOUT THE WORLD BEING TAKEN OVER BY ALIENS. WELLS WROTE IT LONG BEFORE PEOPLE HAD CARS, OR COULD EVEN IMAGINE BUILDING ROCKETS FOR SPACE TRAVEL.

H. G. WELLS

MARK TWAIN (1835-1910) WAS AN AMERICAN FROM MISSOURI. HIS BOOKS ABOUT TOM SAWYER AND HUCKLEBERRY FINN WERE WRITTEN THE WAY PEOPLE ACTUALLY SPOKE. HE ALSO WROTE ABOUT HOW WHITE PEOPLE WERE PREJUDICED AGAINST BLACKS. THIS WAS REVOLUTIONARY AT THE TIME.

MARK TWAIN

SIR ARTHUR CONAN DOYLE (1859-1930) WAS FROM SCOTLAND AND CREATED THE AMAZING DETECTIVE SHERLOCK HOLMES. HOLMES SMOKED A PIPE AND SOLVED MYSTERIES WITH HIS BEST FRIEND, DR. WATSON.

SIR ARTHUR CONAN DOYLE

Stan was not afraid of hard work. He took any job he could get. He wrote for a news company.

He delivered sandwiches. And he worked in the office of a company that made pants.

Even as he worked to help his family, Stan kept writing. And he was getting good at it. A local newspaper sponsored a writing contest. Stan won so many times, the newspaper asked him to stop entering! They wanted someone else to have a chance to win. But the newspaper editor also praised Stan and urged him to do something with his talent. That kind of encouragement meant a lot. Stan would never forget it.

Chapter 2
Becoming Stan Lee

In 1939, when Stan was just sixteen, he graduated from DeWitt Clinton High School. Many kids his age were thinking about college. Not Stan. He needed to keep working. With the help of his cousin Jean, he got a job at Timely, a publishing company run by Martin Goodman.

Mr. Goodman barely knew Stan. "What are you doing here?" Mr. Goodman asked Stan when he showed up for work.

Was Mr. Goodman joking? Had Jean forgotten to mention Stan to her husband? He never got a chance to find out. He was too busy.

Timely published more than two dozen magazines out of its Manhattan offices. Some featured adventure stories set in the Old West; others were about science and health. Stan was assigned to Timely's comics department.

"Some department," Stan joked. "It was Joe and Jack."

Joe was Joe Simon. He was the top editor—the man in charge of all the words on the page. Jack was Jack Kirby. He was the best artist at Timely. These two men were big influences on Stan. But they weren't friendly. When Stan first arrived, they barely looked up.

In those first days on the job, Stan worked as a "gofer"—somebody who does whatever the boss needs. Though he was paid only eight dollars a week, Stan didn't mind. He was proud to be working at Timely.

Stan commuted every day from the Bronx down to Timely's offices on Forty-Second Street. The room Joe and Jack worked in was nothing special. Jack would sit at his drawing board. Joe would pace around the room. Stan sometimes joked that he couldn't see them through all the cigar smoke.

At that time, there was fierce competition from other comic-book companies. DC Comics had created Superman and Batman. Timely's two superheroes were less famous.

The Human Torch was an android created in a lab. He had the power to shoot fire from his hands. He could suddenly burst into flames.

HOW COMICS ARE MADE

A COMIC BOOK IS PUT TOGETHER IN FIVE
MAIN STAGES. THE WRITER CREATES THE STORY.

THE PENCILER ILLUSTRATES THE STORY IN PENCIL
SKETCHES. THEN A LETTERER CAREFULLY PRINTS ALL
THE WORDS OF THE STORY ONTO THE PAGE IN INK.

AT EVERY STAGE, THE EDITOR MAKES SURE THE
WORK IS GOOD ENOUGH TO GO TO THE NEXT STEP.

WHEN READY, THE PAGES GO TO THE INKER.
THESE DAYS, A COMPUTER OFTEN CREATES THICK
INK LINES OVER THE FINISHED PENCIL DRAWINGS.
THE COMIC-BOOK COMPANIES CAN SAVE MONEY
BY USING A COMPUTER INSTEAD OF A PERSON.
BUT EVEN INTO THE 1990S, THE INKER WAS AN
IMPORTANT ARTIST. HIS OR HER JOB WAS TO
TURN PENCIL DRAWINGS INTO DRAMATIC BLACK-
AND-WHITE COMIC ART.

AFTER THE PENCILS ARE INKED, THE COMIC
BOOK IS COLORED AND THEN PRINTED.

But he could not always control those flames. The Sub-Mariner had an even bigger problem. He was the son of a human sea captain and a princess from Atlantis, and he didn't seem to like humans at all!

In 1940, Joe Simon and Jack Kirby created Captain America for Timely Comics. World War II was raging in Europe, and Simon and Kirby were horrified by what they had heard about Adolf Hitler.

Captain America's mission was to fight Nazi Germany. He wore a red, white, and blue costume, the same colors as the American flag. He carried a shield that could stop bullets.

The first issue was a huge success. It sold a million copies. Superman had competition!

That's when Stan got a chance to do more than answer phones. One day, Joe Simon called Stan over. He asked if Stan would be able to write a story for a new issue of Captain America. Stan was thrilled! He turned

in a story called "Captain America Foils the Traitor's Revenge."

Nobody said much about his first story. Stan didn't mind. All that mattered was that Stan got assigned another story right away.

After "The Traitor's Revenge," Stan began to write more. As he wrote, Stan decided to use a pen name instead of his real name. He considered Headline Hunter, Foreign Correspondent, Stan Martine, and even Neels Nats, which was almost "Stan Lee" spelled backward! Stan didn't want to use his full name, Stanley Lieber. "I was saving that for the great American novel," he joked later, "which I never wrote." Finally, he settled on a permanent pen name—Stan Lee— both his names, cut in half.

Chapter 3
The Teenager Takes Over

As Stan was assigned more writing jobs, Joe and Jack were assigned fewer. Mr. Goodman could be difficult. He didn't like to pay the artists much, and they were not happy about it. So Joe and Jack decided to quit.

"I looked around to see who would replace them and I realized, there was nobody," Stan said later. "I was the only guy there."

Stan Lee, Editor

Stan had lots of ideas for stories, but couldn't draw well. So he worked closely with the artists. He also continued as the company's editor, though it was sometimes hard to be an eighteen-year-old boss. Some days, Stan would answer the office door and be asked, "Hey, kid, where can I find Mr. Lee?"

For about a year, Stan ran Timely and wrote whatever Mr. Goodman wanted.

He wrote westerns, mysteries, and horror, and even some romance stories. As much as Stan loved his job, he was distracted. The United States had entered World War II, and Stan wanted to do his part.

He decided to volunteer for the army and reported for duty in the winter of 1942.

WORLD WAR II

THE SECOND WORLD WAR WAS THE BIGGEST WAR IN HISTORY. IT OFFICIALLY BEGAN IN 1939 IN EUROPE. EVERY MAJOR COUNTRY IN THE WORLD WAS INVOLVED, WITH ONE HUNDRED MILLION PEOPLE AROUND THE WORLD SERVING IN MILITARY UNITS. TWO OPPOSING MILITARY ALLIANCES WERE FORMED: THE ALLIES AND THE AXIS.

THE UNITED STATES JOINED THE WAR AFTER A SURPRISE ATTACK BY JAPANESE BOMBERS ON PEARL HARBOR, HAWAII, ON DECEMBER 7, 1941. NEARLY 2,400 SERVICEMEN DIED THAT DAY.

PEARL HARBOR TERRIFIED AMERICANS. BUT IT ALSO INSPIRED THEM. MEN VOLUNTEERED TO GO OVERSEAS AND JOIN THE ALLIES (WHICH INCLUDED ENGLAND, FRANCE, AND THE SOVIET UNION) TO FIGHT THE AXIS (WHICH INCLUDED GERMANY, ITALY, AND JAPAN).

EVEN THOUGH THE ALLIED FORCES WON THE WAR, THE VICTORY CAME AT A GREAT PRICE. MORE THAN FIFTY MILLION PEOPLE DIED BEFORE GERMANY AND JAPAN FINALLY SURRENDERED IN 1945, MAKING WORLD WAR II THE DEADLIEST CONFLICT IN HUMAN HISTORY.

Stan's military classification was "playwright." Because of his work experience, Stan was given a job writing slogans, manuals, and training films for the US government. This was a rare assignment.

Only eight other people have ever been classified as "playwright" by the US Army, including film director Frank Capra, novelist William Saroyan, and Theodor Geisel, better known as Dr. Seuss.

Remarkably, Stan kept working for Timely while he was in the army. The company would mail Stan ideas, and he would send finished stories back to them from wherever he was stationed.

As much as Stan liked serving his country, he was thrilled when the war ended in 1945. He couldn't wait to get back to the world of comic books.

Chapter 4
Joanie

When World War II ended, Stan returned to New York to take over again as Timely's editor. It was a job he would keep for over twenty-five years, until 1972 when he became publisher. Stan was having the time of his life. He rented a two-room apartment in the Almanac Hotel and bought a big white car. It was the first brand-new car he had ever owned!

Then things got even better. A friend wanted to introduce Stan to a model named Betty. His friend thought that Betty and Stan would make a great couple. When Stan showed up at the modeling agency, the most beautiful woman he had ever seen answered the door. There was only one problem: She wasn't Betty. She was a young woman named Joan.

JOAN CLAYTON BOOCOCK

Joan Clayton Boocock had red hair and blue eyes and a great sense of humor. She had moved from England to New York to work as a hat model. In the 1940s, women wore hats every day. And hat models had to be beautiful. Their faces were featured in advertisements in newspapers and magazines.

Stan wasn't one to hold back his feelings.

"I love you," he blurted out that first day. Joan laughed. But she agreed to go on a date.

On December 5, 1947, Stan and Joan became husband and wife. They were married by the same judge who had granted Joan a divorce from her first husband just moments before! Stan wanted to marry Joan quickly, before she could change her mind!

Stan was thrilled and called his beautiful new bride Joanie.

The young couple moved to an apartment close to Timely's offices in Manhattan. The place was so small it barely fit more than their bed. But Stan and Joanie didn't mind. They spent nights out dancing with their friends. Life was great.

Two years later, Stan and Joan moved to a house on Long Island, just outside of New York City. When Stan's mother, Celia, died, his younger brother, Larry, was only fifteen years old. He moved into the new house with Stan and Joanie.

And it's a good thing they had much more space! In 1950, Stan and Joan had a baby girl, Joan Celia. They were heartbroken three years later when a second daughter, Jan, died a few days after she was born. The doctors told Joanie she couldn't have any more children.

Stan loved their daughter, "J.C." He would put her on his shoulders and carry her around their big yard. He took pictures of her with their loving German shepherds, Blackie and Simba. And, in order to spend more time with J.C., Stan tried to work at home as much as possible.

Happy not to be cooped up in Timely's smoke-filled offices, Stan would work outside in the sun. He put his typewriter on a backyard table and worked while standing up. Sometimes, friends would come over and keep Stan company. At other times, J.C. would have her own young friends over to the house.

It was difficult not to notice Stan when he was hard at work. While he wrote comic books, Stan liked to read all the words out loud. It helped him make his superheroes sound right. *Pow! Zap!* He would shout all the most dramatic parts!

J.C.'s friends sometimes wondered why her father was making all that noise. J.C. told them not to worry. That was just her father at work.

Chapter 5
Comics Under Attack

Not everybody loved comics as much as Stan did. Starting in the early 1940s, some adults complained that comic books were bad for children. Why? They were filled with violence, bloody details, and horrific stories. People were afraid that comics would influence young people in dangerous ways.

In 1948, angry parents even held public comic-book burnings in Binghamton, New York,

and Spencer, West Virginia. And in 1949, the very popular *Family Circle* magazine published a story called "What Can You Do about Comic Books?" The article told parents they needed to read comic books before their children did to make sure they were "safe" and not too violent.

Stan and the other comic-book creators didn't take the complaints very seriously. Business was still very good.

But in 1954, Fredric Wertham, a child psychologist, wrote a book called *Seduction of the Innocent*. Dr. Wertham said that comics were dangerous to children. His ideas led to congressional hearings in Washington, DC, about whether to outlaw comic books. Some stores even stopped selling them to children!

The congressional hearings had a huge impact on sales. Fifteen comic-book companies went out of business in 1954 alone.

The remaining publishers did their best to survive. Together, they founded the Comics Code Authority.

They wrote their own rules to make sure comic books didn't include stories that would upset parents or politicians.

The Comics Code Authority had to approve every comic book before it was printed. If approved, the comic could use the Comics Code Seal of Approval on its front cover. That meant it was "safe" for children to read.

THE COMICS CODE AUTHORITY

THE COMICS CODE AUTHORITY ESTABLISHED THAT COMIC BOOKS WOULD:

- SHOW RESPECT FOR AUTHORITY (SUCH AS THE POLICE).
- ENSURE THAT GOOD WOULD ALWAYS TRIUMPH OVER EVIL.
- NOT USE THE WORDS "TERROR" OR "HORROR."
- SHOW NO VAMPIRES, WEREWOLVES, GHOULS, OR ZOMBIES!

APPROVED BY THE COMICS CODE AUTHORITY

STAN FOLLOWED THE CODE FOR YEARS. IN 1971, THE US GOVERNMENT ASKED STAN TO CREATE A SPIDER-MAN COMIC ABOUT THE DANGERS OF DRUGS AND DRUG USE. BUT THE COMICS CODE AUTHORITY DIDN'T ALLOW COMIC BOOKS TO EVEN MENTION DRUGS! STAN IGNORED THE CODE AND PUBLISHED THREE ANTI-DRUG ISSUES FEATURING SPIDER-MAN.

THEY DIDN'T GET A SEAL OF APPROVAL. STILL, THE COMICS WERE A HIT. STAN NOW KNEW HE COULD MAKE HIS OWN RULES. IN 2001, MARVEL DID JUST THAT, OFFICIALLY WITHDRAWING FROM THE COMICS CODE AUTHORITY AND CREATING ITS OWN RATING SYSTEM.

Chapter 6
Marvel Is Born

By 1960, Stan had been working on comic books for twenty years. But he really wasn't having much fun anymore. Comic books were not selling. Kids were more interested in television shows and rock-and-roll music than old superheroes. Even Captain America was canceled due to low sales.

Stan couldn't help thinking of the good old days with Jack Kirby in the smoky rooms at Timely. He missed the old team and the excitement he used to feel when he came to work. He told Joanie that he was going to quit. He was planning to stomp into Mr. Goodman's office and tell him that he was through with comics.

There was only one problem.

Just when he was ready to quit, Mr. Goodman offered Stan an exciting new challenge. A rival company, DC Comics, had just put out a comic book: the *Justice League of America.*

Instead of just one superhero, the comic book included seven of them working as a team: Superman, Batman, Wonder Woman, Flash, Green Lantern, Aquaman, and the Martian Manhunter!

Justice League comics were flying off the shelf.

Mr. Goodman asked Stan to create his own team. He even suggested bringing back Captain America and the Human Torch.

When Stan told Joanie about Mr. Goodman's idea, she told Stan that she would always support him. She knew her husband better than anybody. She knew he loved a creative challenge.

"You know, Stan," Joanie said, "if Martin wants you to create a new group of superheroes, this could be a chance for you to do it in a way you've always wanted to."

By that, she meant that Stan had nothing to lose. If he took too much of a risk and annoyed Mr. Goodman, he might get fired. That wouldn't matter to Stan because he had already planned to quit! But if he came up with something special, he might please Mr. Goodman and recapture the excitement of his early days at Timely.

Stan didn't want to just bring back old characters. He wanted to create new ones. His new team would not be perfectly handsome like Superman or incredibly strong like Captain America. They would have the normal problems and weaknesses of regular people. Their lives would not always be easy.

And Stan knew exactly who could help: his old partner Jack.

JACK KIRBY

JACK KIRBY WAS BORN ON AUGUST 28, 1917.
WHEN HE WAS JUST FOURTEEN, HE BEGAN TAKING
CLASSES AT ART SCHOOL. SOON AFTER, HE HAD TO
QUIT SCHOOL WHEN HIS FATHER LOST HIS JOB.

JACK WAS A VERY GOOD ARTIST. AT TIMELY AND LATER AT MARVEL COMICS, JACK HELPED CREATE CAPTAIN AMERICA, THE FANTASTIC FOUR, AND OTHER IMPORTANT SUPERHEROES. THEY CALLED HIM "KING" KIRBY. BUT JACK DIDN'T LIKE NICKNAMES. HE LIKED GETTING CREDIT FOR HIS WORK. HE THOUGHT THAT STAN HOGGED THE SPOTLIGHT, AND HE GREW BITTER ABOUT NOT BEING GIVEN ENOUGH ATTENTION FOR THE CHARACTERS HE CREATED. HE WONDERED WHY SO MANY ARTICLES MENTIONED ONLY STAN.

STAN TOLD EVERYONE THAT JACK HAD CREATED THE CHARACTERS WITH HIM. BUT BY THE TIME HE DIED IN 1994, JACK FELT CHEATED AND HADN'T TALKED TO STAN FOR YEARS.

JACK KIRBY IS REMEMBERED AS ONE OF THE GREATEST COMIC-BOOK ARTISTS OF ALL TIME.

It had been years since Jack had quit his regular job at Timely Comics. But starting in 1958, Jack had been taking assignments from Stan. Now, Stan needed something more. He needed Jack's help in creating a new generation of comic-book heroes.

The Fantastic Four were led by the brilliant scientist Reed Richards. Sue Storm hoped to marry Reed one day. Sue's younger brother, Johnny Storm, was the third member of the team. But Stan and Jack's greatest creation was the final member of the Fantastic Four:

Ben Grimm. Ben was a military pilot who was a friend of Reed's.

It was Reed's dream to travel to outer space. He built a spacecraft and invited Ben, Sue, and Johnny along. Once in space, they were blasted by radiation, which gave each of them special powers.

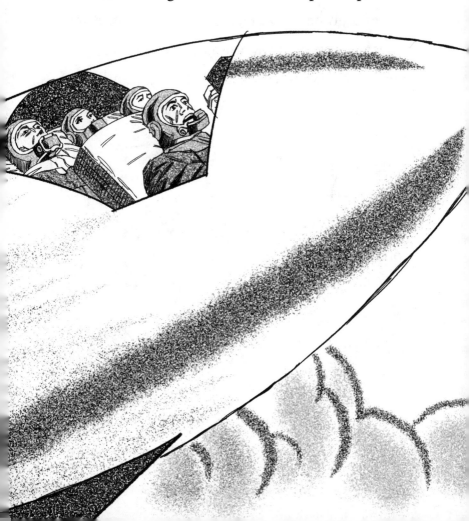

But Ben became deformed. The radiation turned him into a giant creature with an orange, rock-like skin. Depressed, Ben renamed himself The Thing.

The Thing was a new kind of superhero. He grumbled and rolled his eyes. He wished he could go back to being his normal self. But he was incredibly loyal and also believed in fighting crime. Reed became the bigmouthed Mr. Fantastic. Sue Storm became the Invisible Girl. Johnny Storm, who could now burst into flames at will, became the new Human Torch.

When the first comic book was published in 1961, readers loved the Fantastic Four!

Their success convinced Stan that he had made the right decision to take on Mr. Goodman's challenge. It also gave him the confidence to create other unlikely heroes.

As a boy, Stan had read Robert Louis Stevenson's *The Strange Case of Dr. Jekyll and Mr. Hyde*. The book told the story of one man with two very different personalities. Dr. Jekyll was a very good person, but as Mr. Hyde, he was evil.

For the new character, Stan came up with his own version of Dr. Jekyll and Mr. Hyde. Dr. Bruce Banner was a mild-mannered scientist. But when he lost his temper or felt panicked, he turned into a green monster: the Hulk.

The Hulk first appeared in 1962 in *The Incredible Hulk #1* and became instantly popular among comic-book fans.

Stan's next comic team was a group of outcast mutants called the X-Men. Professor Xavier,

their mentor, showed them that
they also could be heroes.

Stan was on a roll, but was
very busy and needed help.
He had the perfect guy for the
job. He called in his younger
brother, Larry. Larry Lieber
had gone to art school and
done some writing for Stan. Now they began
to work together more closely. Over the next two
years, Stan and Larry would help create two of
their most popular characters, Thor and Iron Man.

When Larry got tired of drawing those characters, he launched a western series called Rawhide Kid.

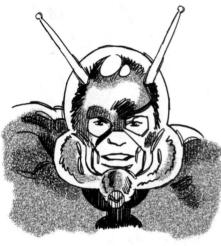

Stan kept coming up with new characters, including Daredevil and Ant-Man.

With so much success, Stan decided to make a big change.

In the 1950s, Mr. Goodman had changed Timely's name to Atlas Comics. But Stan had thought the company needed a fresher name. Times were changing. Stan was developing comics with a new style and approach. Although he had gone back to using superheroes, this new wave of crime fighters was different. They had issues! They sometimes struggled with their superpowers and longed for their days as mere humans. Stan remembered the title used in one of the early comic books published by Timely: Marvel. He liked the sound of that! And Mr. Goodman agreed.

Stan gave his crew of artists and writers at Marvel Comics nicknames and called the team his "bullpen." The writers, artists, and inkers worked in the main room at Marvel. Stan wanted Marvel's readers to imagine the company as a big clubhouse where everybody hung out, told jokes, and developed amazing comic books.

If readers had a question, they could send a letter directly to Stan. He would answer those letters on a page he put in every comic book called "Bullpen Bulletins." Stan had fun writing these pages. He gave each Bulletin a funny-sounding title at the top of the page, like

"More mirthful, monumental, mind-staggering memoranda from your Marvel madmen!" Stan wrote an open letter to readers called "Stan's Soapbox" and came up with his own favorite terms, like "'nuff said" and "Excelsior!"

Other comic-book companies were "Brand *Echh*," Stan joked. Marvel Comics was king.

M.M.M.S.

MARVEL COMICS' IN-HOUSE FAN CLUB WAS LAUNCHED IN FEBRUARY 1965. CALLED THE "MERRY MARVEL MARCHING SOCIETY" (OR M.M.M.S., FOR SHORT), THE CLUB INCLUDED VARIOUS RANKS SUCH AS Q.N.S. (QUITE 'NUFF SAYER) AND F.F.F. (FEARLESS FRONT-FACER). FOR THE ONE-DOLLAR MEMBERSHIP FEE, CLUB MEMBERS WOULD RECEIVE A WELCOME LETTER, A MEMBERSHIP CARD, STICKERS, BUTTONS, AND A ONE-SIDED RECORD CALLED *THE VOICES OF MARVEL* FEATURING STAN, THE GUYS OF THE BULLPEN, AND STAN'S SECRETARY, "FABULOUS FLO" STEINBERG.

IN 1969, THE M.M.M.S. WAS ABSORBED INTO THE LARGER FAN CLUB, MARVELMANIA INTERNATIONAL.

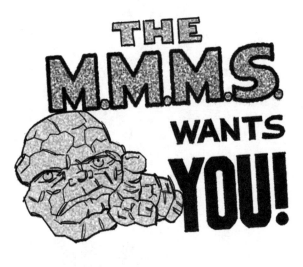

Chapter 7
Spider-Man

Even with
the company's
new name
and newfound
success, Stan
had trouble
explaining his
latest idea to
Mr. Goodman.
Who would
be interested in
a skinny teenager who
could stick to ceilings like a
fly? "Spider-Man"? Didn't Stan
realize that people hated spiders?

Stan said he came up with the idea for
Spider-Man after watching a fly climb up a wall.

How about a superhero who could stick to things?
Stan struggled to come up with a good name.
Fly-Man or Insect-Man didn't sound right. Then,
Stan thought of Spider-Man. That could work!

He originally wanted to ask artist Jack Kirby to draw the new character, but decided that Jack's drawings were not right. Jack made Spider-Man look too heroic, too powerful.

Spider-Man was really Peter Parker, a geeky teenager who was unsure of himself. He got pushed around in school by a football star named Flash Thompson. Then a radioactive spider bit Peter and gave him special powers. The shy boy could suddenly stick to walls and ceilings as if he had suction cups for hands. He was also super strong.

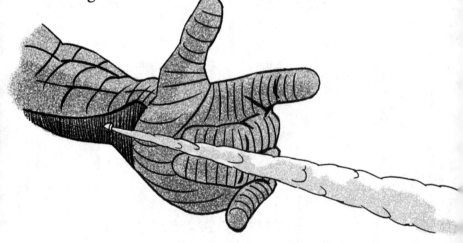

STEVE DITKO

To create this new superhero, Stan found an artistic partner in Steve Ditko. Steve himself was awkward and shy and didn't like to go to parties. He had no problem making Peter Parker different. He would not be a giant, muscle-bound hero. But when Peter transformed into Spider-Man, he was drawn like a classic superhero, with a new "look" and costume designed by Steve.

Spider-Man first appeared in a comic book in June 1962, and he was the perfect character for Stan's new approach: regular people who happen to become superheroes. The Marvel characters would have flaws and problems.

But ultimately, they would devote themselves to fighting crime.

Despite Mr. Goodman's doubts, the first comic book to feature Spider-Man was popular. In fact, Marvel's new group of superheroes sold thirteen million comic books in 1962—nearly double the amount they sold the previous year!

Stan had been part of the "Golden Age of Comics" in the 1940s. Now he was part creator of the "Silver Age," which lasted roughly from 1956–1970. Comic fans sometimes refer to this popular return to superheroes—and away from crime and romance stories—as the "Silver Sixties" and even "The Marvel Age."

Who said nobody likes spiders?

SOME OF MARVEL'S BIGGEST VILLAINS

DOCTOR DOOM IS AN INVENTOR AND A SORCERER WHO IS THE ARCHENEMY OF THE FANTASTIC FOUR.

GALACTUS, FROM THE PLANET TAA, IS SO POWERFUL HE CAN EAT ENTIRE PLANETS.

THE GREEN GOBLIN, ONE OF SPIDER-MAN'S ENEMIES, IS A HALLOWEEN-THEMED SUPERVILLAIN WHOSE WEAPONS INCLUDE BATS, GHOSTS, AND EXPLODING JACK-O-LANTERNS.

ULTRON'S OUTER ARMOR IS SO POWERFUL, HE IS ALMOST INDESTRUCTIBLE. HE IS ALSO A GENIUS.

THANOS IS A MUTANT WHO CAN TRAVEL THROUGH SPACE WITH A SPECIAL CHAIR. HE USES HIS SUPERHUMAN STRENGTH TO BATTLE IRON MAN, THE THING, AND SPIDER-MAN.

LOKI IS BOTH THOR'S ADOPTED BROTHER—
AND HIS SWORN ENEMY. HIS FULL NAME IS
LOKI LAUFEYSON.

VENOM, A LIQUID-LIKE ALIEN LOOKING FOR
A HUMAN HOST, IS ONE OF SPIDER-MAN'S
ARCHENEMIES.

MAGNETO WAS BORN ON
EARTH WITH SPECIAL POWERS.
HE BECAME A VILLAIN AFTER
HIS FAMILY DIED DURING
WORLD WAR II AND HE
DECIDED MUTANTS NEEDED
TO BE DEFENDED.

ONSLAUGHT WAS CREATED FROM THE COMBINED
SOULS OF PROFESSOR X AND MAGNETO. HE
BATTLES BOTH THE HULK AND THE X-MEN.

Chapter 8
Movie Stardom for Marvel

With Marvel Comics now making so much
money, Mr. Goodman
decided it was time to sell.
A man named Martin
Ackerman bought the
company in 1968 with
one condition: Stan
Lee had to remain
in charge.

Stan did. By
now, Stan was the
face of Marvel.
While the artists
tended to keep
to themselves,

Stan's outgoing nature made him a natural spokesman for the company. He spoke at colleges and conventions. He posed for magazines and newspapers. Stan also had developed his distinctive look. He grew an identifiable mustache and always wore sunglasses, even when he was inside!

In 1972, when Mr. Goodman officially retired as publisher, Stan got a promotion. He became the publisher of Marvel. Roy Thomas, a writer who had been working on X-Men, became Marvel's editor. As publisher, Stan could focus on new ideas.

Stan wanted the Marvel characters to branch out into television shows and movies.

Television was easy. In 1977, *The Incredible Hulk* made its premiere on TV. Stan was not in charge of the show, but he did have an important role. The producers of *The Incredible Hulk* wanted the Hulk to be red, not green. Stan said no. The Hulk had to be green. *The Incredible Hulk* ran for more than eighty episodes over five years!

Stan had a tougher time getting Marvel into the movies. For years, movie producers had refused to turn comic books into movies. They worried that it would be too difficult to show illustrated comic-book action using real actors. In 1978, everything changed when the movie *Superman* came out. Actor Christopher Reeve played Superman.

The movie earned $300 million worldwide, the sixth highest-grossing film ever at that time. *Superman* convinced Hollywood that superhero movies could work.

Stan began to meet with Hollywood producers, and in 1980, he and Joanie moved to Los Angeles.

They bought a house in West Hollywood overlooking the Sunset Strip, a glamorous part of the city full of stores, restaurants, and rock clubs. It was so exciting! Stan and Joanie loved Hollywood. They made new friends in California. J.C. worked as a model and began painting. Her parents were thrilled to go to her first art show.

As much as Stan loved California, he found it wasn't easy to get movies made. Producers argued. They sued each other. At one point writers had written eight different scripts for a movie version of Spider-Man. Nobody was satisfied.

Director James Cameron wanted to make a Spider-Man movie. But it was taking too long. He made movies like *Terminator* and *Titanic* instead.

In 1989, a movie about Marvel's character the Punisher was filmed, but never released in movie theaters. Neither was 1994's version of the Fantastic Four.

The struggles in Hollywood caught Stan by surprise. Back in New York, Marvel Comics was also having problems. Ackerman had sold Marvel in 1986, and the new owners wanted to expand.

The company tried to get too big, too fast. They bought a baseball-card company and a sticker company. Both lost money.

Finally, in 1996, Marvel went bankrupt. The company was broke.

But Stan never gave up. He knew the Marvel family of characters would someday find new fans on the big screen. He also knew that Marvel needed him. Everybody knew Stan Lee! To relaunch Marvel, the new owners came up with a plan.

They created a department within Marvel that was devoted exclusively to making movies. They called it Marvel Studios.

AVI ARAD

A man named Avi Arad was put in charge.

Avi had grown up in Israel reading Spider-Man comic books translated into Hebrew. He was thrilled to have Stan giving him advice.

With Avi in charge, Marvel finally began to get films made. *Blade* came first, in 1998, based on a superhero who hunted vampires. The movie starred Wesley Snipes and earned $131 million around the world.

The first X-Men movie came out in 2000 and was even bigger. Critics loved it, and crowds flocked to theaters. *X-Men* earned $200 million. The film also featured Stan's first appearance in a Marvel film. He played a hot-dog salesman! Two years later, *Spider-Man* was finally released. The movie starred Tobey Maguire as Peter Parker,

Willem Dafoe as the Green Goblin,
and Kirsten Dunst as Mary Jane Watson. It was a
worldwide hit, earning $822 million!

After twenty years in Hollywood, Stan was finally seeing his dreams for Marvel come true.

STAN LEE'S MOVIE ROLES

THE DISTINGUISHED GENTLEMAN WITH THE WHITE MUSTACHE WHO APPEARS FOR JUST A MINUTE IN SO MANY SUPERHERO MOVIES IS STAN LEE. STAN APPEARS IN WHAT IS CALLED A "CAMEO" ROLE. A CAMEO USUALLY INVOLVES SOMEBODY FAMOUS PLAYING A VERY TINY ROLE. HERE ARE A FEW OF STAN'S MOST FAMOUS CAMEOS:

FANTASTIC FOUR—WILLIE LUMPKIN, THE MAILMAN (A CHARACTER STAN HAD CREATED FOR THE *FANTASTIC FOUR* COMIC BOOKS)

X-MEN—HOT-DOG VENDOR

HULK—SECURITY GUARD

IRON MAN 3—BEAUTY PAGEANT JUDGE

SPIDER-MAN 3—MAN READING A NEWS TICKER. (HE EVEN GETS TO SAY ONE OF HIS FAVORITE LINES, "'NUFF SAID.")

THOR: THE DARK WORLD—PATIENT IN A MENTAL HOSPITAL

AVENGERS: INFINITY WAR—PETER PARKER'S SCHOOL BUS DRIVER

Stan loved *Spider-Man,* but Marvel's biggest movie success was still to come.

Iron Man came out in 2008, with Robert Downey Jr. starring as the billionaire adventurer Tony Stark. Stan thought Robert Downey Jr. was born to play Stark! The actor was perfect for the role. *Iron Man* was such a smash, it led to two sequels.

ROBERT DOWNEY JR.

In 2013, *Iron Man 3* earned $1.2 billion around the world, making it the fifth highest-grossing film at that time.

Black Panther broke many box-office records in 2018 and went on to become the highest-grossing film by a black director, Ryan Coogler.

And later that same year, *Avengers: Infinity War* smashed all expectations to become the very first superhero movie to earn $2 billion worldwide.

In 2019, *Black Panther* became the first film from Marvel Studios to ever win an Academy Award! It won three awards for Costume Design, Production Design, and Original Score (Music).

"I think Marvel will end up being the biggest company in showbiz," Stan said in an interview.

Chapter 9
Legacy

Some people retire when they get older. They pick up their golf clubs or take a cruise. Not Stan.

"I think if you enjoy what you do it's like playing and you can't stop," he told an interviewer. "It's so much fun." He was eighty-nine when he said that!

Though Stan stepped down as Marvel's publisher in the 1990s, he continued to serve as an executive producer of the many movies that featured his characters. Not that he needed the work. Creating some of the world's most popular comic-book characters has made him very rich.

But Stan was never overly concerned with money. He loved dreaming up new ideas. As he got older, he tried new things. He even went to

work for the competition! For years, DC Comics
was Marvel's biggest rival. In 2001, DC Comics
asked Stan to write stories featuring the DC
superheroes. Stan's *Just Imagine . . .*
series included Superman,
Batman, Wonder Woman, and
other DC characters.

"As long as I can keep busy," he wrote, "it saves me from dwelling too much on the past."

And boy, did Stan keep busy! He created other companies, started his own YouTube channel, and narrated a series of video games. He also made regular appearances at comic conventions. In fact, whenever he appeared, tickets sold out within minutes! Stan became a living legend. Millions of people have read comic books and seen movies starring his characters. Marvel has even created a Stan Lee action figure.

Stan loved his work and always cherished his family. He and Joan were married for seventy years!

And J.C. stayed close to her parents. She was often seen walking down the red carpet with her father at movie premieres.

Stan and his younger brother, Larry, continued to work together on the version of Spider-Man that is printed on the comics page in hundreds of newspapers each day.

And in 2010, Stan started hosting his own television show, *Stan Lee's Superhumans*. And in an interview just after his ninetieth birthday, he got excited as he talked about future Marvel plans, mentioning movies about Doctor Strange, Ant-Man, and Guardians of the Galaxy.

He regrettably had to cancel a sold-out appearance at a comics convention in Denver. But it wasn't because he was too tired or too old. It was because Hollywood needed him. *The Amazing Spider-Man 2* was filming, and it was time for Stan's next cameo.

As Stan would say, "What could be more fun?"

Stan Lee passed away on November 12, 2018. He was ninety-five years old.

TIMELINE OF STAN LEE'S LIFE

1922 — Stanley Lieber is born on December 28 in New York City

1939 — Stan joins Timely Comics as an assistant

1941 — Stan's first comic-book story appears in *Captain America Comics #3*. Later that year, Stan takes over as editor at Timely.

1942 — Stan joins the US Army

1945 — Stan returns to Timely Comics after finishing his military service

1947 — Stan marries Joan Clayton Boocock

1950 — Stan and Joan's daughter Joan Celia ("J.C.") is born

1951 — Timely Comics is renamed Atlas Comics

1961 — Stan and Jack Kirby create the Fantastic Four, their first superhero team. Atlas Comics renamed Marvel Comics.

1965 — Stan launches Marvel's "Bullpen Bulletins," which includes his open letter to readers, called "Stan's Soapbox"

1971 — Stan agrees to do Spider-Man storyline with anti-drug message at request of US government

1980 — Stan moves to Los Angeles to develop movies for Marvel Comics

1994 — Stan is inducted into the Will Eisner Hall of Fame, a special honor for comic-book creators

1998 — *Blade*, starring Wesley Snipes, is Marvel's first movie hit

2002 — First *Spider-Man* movie is released (*Spider-Man 2* [2004], *Spider-Man 3* [2007], and *The Amazing Spider-Man* [2012] follow)

2008 — First *Iron Man* movie is released (*Iron Man 2* [2010] and *Iron Man 3* [2013] follow)

2012 — *Stan Lee: With Great Power* documentary is released

2018 — Dies November 12, age ninety-five

TIMELINE OF THE WORLD

Stock market crash leads to the Great Depression	1929
Japan attacks American military base at Pearl Harbor, leading United States to enter World War II	1941
World War II ends	1945
Jackie Robinson becomes the first African American to play in the major leagues	1947
Elvis Presley's "Heartbreak Hotel" becomes his first number one hit	1956
Neil Armstrong is the first man to walk on the moon	1969
HBO becomes the first pay-television channel	1972
The Vietnam War comes to an end	1975
Apple releases its first Macintosh personal computer	1984
The fall of the Berlin Wall marks the end of the Cold War	1989
The first Harry Potter novel is published	1997
Apple releases the first line of iPod music players	2001
Mark Zuckerberg and a group of friends found Facebook	2004
First successful face transplant surgery takes place in Turkey	2012
Cristiano Ronaldo of Real Madrid C.F. wins the FIFA Ballon d'Or for best player of the year	2016
"Bomb Cyclone" hits the Northeastern United States, flooding the New York City subway system	2018

BIBLIOGRAPHY

Broverman, Aaron. "Stan Lee Talks the Future of Comics, Comic Book Movies and Superheroes." **Moviefone.com**. August 26, 2010.

Duncan, Randy, and Matthew J. Smith. **The Power of Comics: History, Form and Culture**. New York: Continuum, 2009.

Gitlin, Martin. **Stan Lee: Comic Book Superhero (Essential Lives)**. Minneapolis: Abdo Publishing, 2009.

Howe, Sean. **Marvel Comics: The Untold Story**. New York: Harper Perennial, 2013.

Irving, Christopher. **Leaping Tall Buildings: The Origins of American Comics**. Brooklyn: Powerhouse, 2012.

Lee, Stan. **Marvel Visionaries**. New York: Marvel Comics, 2005.

Lee, Stan, and George Mair. **Excelsior!: The Amazing Life of Stan Lee**. New York: Touchstone, 2002.

McLaughlin, Jeff (editor). **Stan Lee: Conversations (Conversations with Comic Artists)**. Jackson, MS: University Press of Mississippi, 2007.

Raphael, Jordan. **Stan Lee and the Rise and Fall of the American Comic Book**. Chicago: Chicago Review Press, 2003.

Smith, Jordan. "Marvel Might Need to Get A Little Crazy: Stan Lee Talks Future Films." **Hollywood.com**. September 18, 2013.